caring
for us

I am a
Doctor

Deborah Chancellor

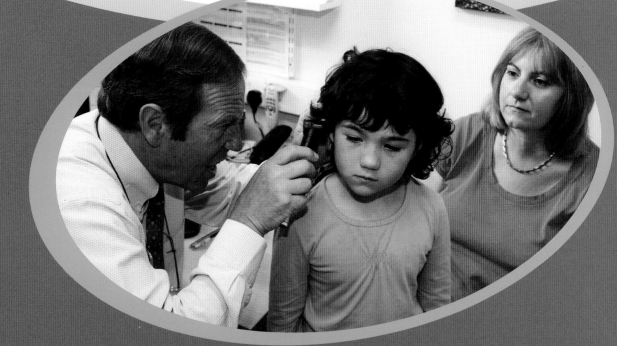

FRANKLIN WATTS
LONDON • SYDNEY

First published in 2010
by Franklin Watts

Copyright © Franklin Watts 2010

Franklin Watts
338 Euston Road
London NW1 3BH

Franklin Watts Australia
Level 17/207 Kent Street
Sydney, NSW 2000

Series editor: Jeremy Smith
Art director: Jonathan Hair
Design: Elaine Wilkinson
Photography: Chris Fairclough

Thanks to Dr Bertram, Hazel, Eileen, Liz, Izzy, Su, Josh and all the staff at Linton Health Centre.

Dewey number: 610.6'95

ISBN: 978 0 7496 9515 6

Printed in China

Franklin Watts is a division of Hachette Children's Books,
an Hachette UK company.
www.hachette.co.uk

Contents

Words in **bold** are in the glossary on page 24.

My job

I am a doctor.
People come to see
me at my **surgery** when
they are not feeling well.
I help them to
get better.

What do you think?

How
can doctors
help their
patients
get well?

4

I work at a health centre in
a village called Linton.

In the surgery

If someone wants to see me, they phone the health centre to make an appointment with the receptionist.

What do you think?

Why do you need to book to see a doctor?

6

My patient list tells me who is coming to see me that day. I check the **patient notes** on my computer.

Seeing patients

Every day, I see about 35 patients. When they arrive, they sit in the waiting room until it is their turn to see me.

What do you think?

What do you think the doctor is doing in this picture?

In my surgery, I ask my patients how they are feeling and try to help them to relax.

9

What's wrong?

Sometimes I examine my patient to see what is wrong. I may listen to their heart and lungs with a stethoscope.

I may look in my patient's ears, and take their temperature with a **thermometer**.

The right medicine

If a patient needs **medicine** to help them get better, I give them a **prescription**.

Do you know?

Never take medicine unless a trusted adult gives it to you.

The patient takes the prescription to a **pharmacy**, to pick up the right medicine.

13

Emergency visit

Sometimes people come to the surgery if they have had an accident, or become ill quickly.

What do you think?

Where else could you go in an emergency?

They may need to be taken to hospital to get the right **treatment**. For example, if a patient has a broken arm, they may need a plaster cast.

On the phone

I talk to some patients on the phone if they can't get out to the surgery, but need my advice.

What do you think?

When do you think it's helpful to speak to a doctor by phone?

16

When I am not with my patients, I have a
lot of paperwork to do in my surgery.

Out and about

I leave the surgery to visit patients
at home if they can't come out
to see me.

18

I take my medical case with me when I do a home visit. It contains everything I need.

What do you think?

What kind of patients might need a home visit?

Meeting together

Every day, I meet the other doctors at the surgery to talk about our work.

We work at different times. When I go home at the end of the day, another doctor takes over at evening surgery.

What do you think?

Why do doctors need to talk about their work?

21

Look after yourself

Eat healthy food to help you stay well. This way you might not have to visit the doctor very often.

What do you think?

What kind of foods are good for you to eat?

Take lots of exercise to keep fit and strong.
Get plenty of sleep, so your body can rest
and fight germs.

23

Glossary

germs tiny living things that can make you ill

medicine something you take to help you get better

patient notes information about a patient's medical treatment

pharmacy a place where you can pick up medicine

prescription a doctor's request for medicine

stethoscope a piece of equipment used by a doctor to listen to your heart and lungs

surgery the room where a doctor sees patients

thermometer equipment for measuring your temperature

treatment medical care to help you get better

Index